Collins

# Enhanced English Alive Workbook 3

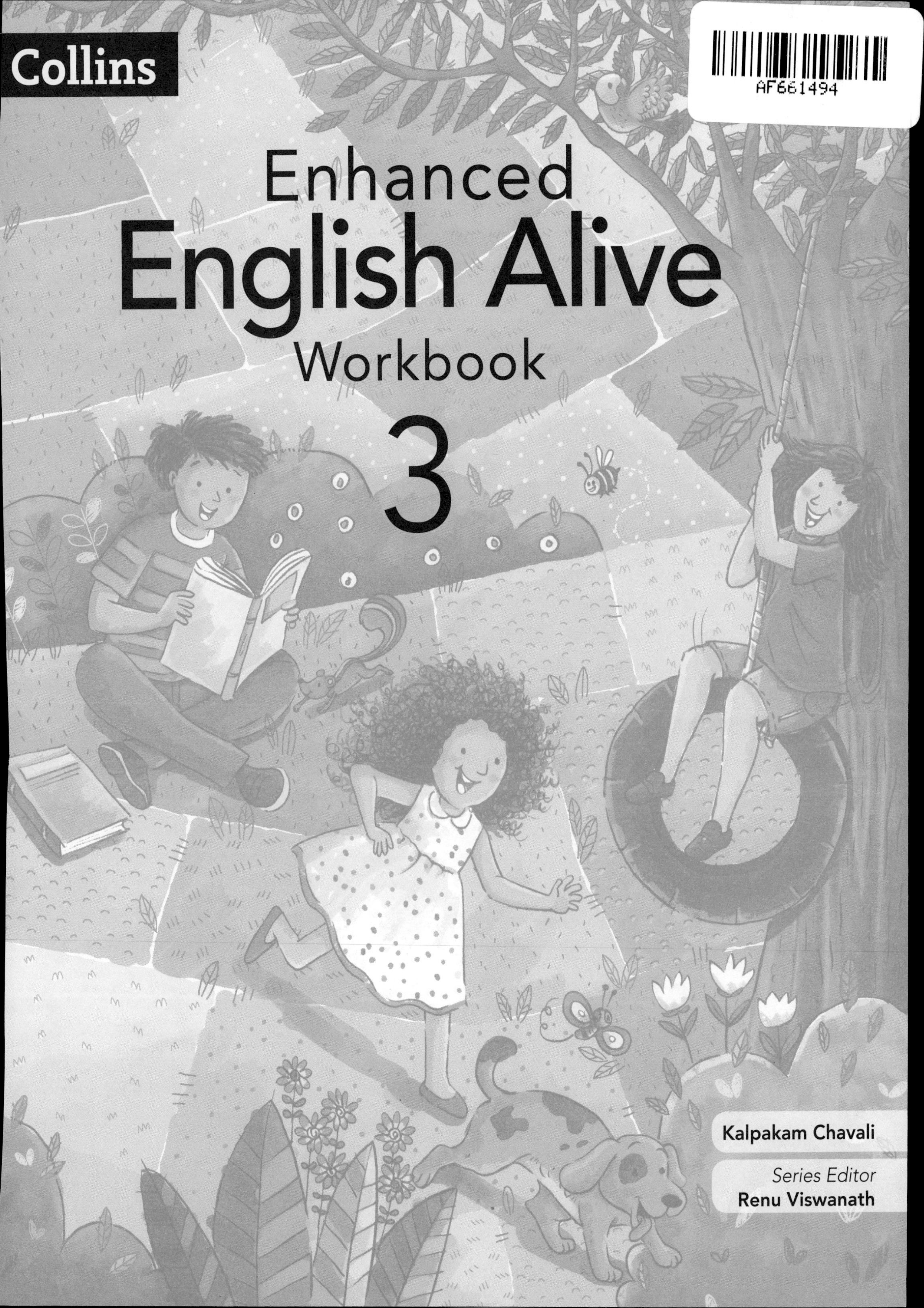

Kalpakam Chavali

*Series Editor*
**Renu Viswanath**

# Acknowledgements

**Cover and Title Page:** Created by Toonfantasy

**Inside: Page 10:** bandian1122, kbeis; **16:** tonybilge; **17:** KaterinaKr, ayutaka, Dezein suryazaidan, nataka; **19:** passengerz, Smokeyjo, ARTPUPPY; **20:** Ylivdesign; **26:** bubaone, colematt; **30:** Tomacco; **31:** THEPALMER; **33:** ElenaNayashkova, elenabs, Hulinska_Yevheniia, Nocturnus; **34:** Pitris, scotellaro, NiwatSingsamarn, katrina-happy, Tigatelu; **36:** viyadaistock, nidwlw, polygraphus, cyfrogclone, Ekaterina_Vitchenko, Agatalina; **48:** nsj-images, johnwoodcock, Jane_Kelly, Eloku; **50:** nokee; **52:** Mark Murphy, pijama61, graphic-bee, clairevis; **53:** Tigatelu, Victor_Brave; **56:** colematt, Elena Belous, blueringmedia, Hein Nouwens, eliflamra; **58:** John T. Daniels; **63:** RUSSELLTATEdotCOM, smartboy10, seamartini, madebymarco, mattasbestos; **65:** myillo, myillo; **74:** velusariot

# Preface

***Enhanced English Alive*** is a multi-skill course in English that adheres to the guidelines laid down by the **National Education Policy, 2020**. This edition retains the original essence of teaching communicative English using a cross-curricular approach and interactive and experiential teaching and learning methods. It offers high-quality English language materials with a coherent structured approach, effective integration of subject knowledge and life skills.

The series comprises Coursebooks and Workbooks for Foundational Stage (Nursery, LKG, UKG, Classes 1 and 2), Preparatory Stage (Classes 3 to 5), and Middle Stage (Classes 6 to 8). Literature Readers are for the Preparatory and Middle Stages (Classes 3 to 8). Each grade package includes a Teacher's Resource Pack and a Collins DigiSuite.

This series integrates the essence of **NIPUN Bharat** guidelines, which extensively deal with foundational literacy and numeracy. Each book aims to motivate learners to read independently, to improve their vocabulary, to develop their critical thinking and creative skills, as well as to enhance their ability to express themselves both verbally and in writing.

This series takes care of the requirements of **Structured Assessments For Analyzing Learning (SAFAL)**. Research-based activities and projects have been used to instill inquiry-based learning, while comprehension passages have been followed by extrapolative and value-based questions that involve analysis-based learning.

## Key features

### Coursebooks

Each Coursebook has a wide variety of texts from various genres carefully selected from both Indian and Western literature. The books aim at cross-curricular teaching, covering topics included in the syllabus of other subjects taught in the respective grades. They also inculcate mindfulness in learners in the Foundational and Preparatory stages (Classes 1 to 5), in addition to language skills. A lot of interesting and engaging activities are used as tools to teach language skills. Additionally, in the Middle Stage (Classes 6 to 8), an end-of-year Assessment Paper has been provided.

### Workbooks

- **Reading:** Each Workbook has 8 to 11 comprehension passages which include prose and poems. Exercises with a variety of questions follow these passages and aim to provide ample practice for the learners.
- **Vocabulary:** A variety of exercises and activities on vocabulary topics mapped with the corresponding Coursebook are given to reinforce the concepts. Exercises on spelling and pronunciation have also been provided to allow a thorough revision of these linguistic rules.
- **Grammar:** Grammar concepts taught in the Coursebooks are reinforced with summarised explanations and graded exercises.
- **Listening and Speaking:** More innovative activities and communicative tasks have been provided to practice and improve the listening and speaking skills of the learners.
- **Writing:** This well-graded section has a variety of creative-writing exercises.

- **Activities:** A fun activity is given at the end of each poem and some prose pieces in order to make learning an interactive and enjoyable experience for young learners.
- **Test papers:** Short assessment papers provide a great opportunity to the learners to revise the concepts of vocabulary and grammar taught in each unit. Each paper evaluates the concepts covered in a group of chapters.

## Literature Readers

The Literature Readers teach critical appreciation of literature through short stories, folktales, fairytales, poems, and extracts from classics from the literature of different ages. The summary of each chapter helps in imbibing the essence of the text. Literary devices are also taught along with a glossary of literary terms.

## Teacher's Resource Pack

The Teacher's Resource Pack contain model lesson plans, additional worksheets, and grammar-based projects covering all the pedagogical aspects included in the Coursebooks, along with listening texts and answer keys to all exercises across Coursebooks, Workbooks, Literature Readers, and additional assessment papers.

# Detailed Contents

| Chapter | Reading Comprehension | Vocabulary | Grammar |
|---|---|---|---|
| 1. Limericks | | • Rhyming words<br>• Limerick | |
| 2. Birbal Identifies the Thief | Factual, inferential | • Singular and plural<br>• Countable and uncountable nouns | • Nouns: common noun, proper noun, and collective noun |
| 3. Think Hard, Boatman | Factual, inferential and extrapolative | • Word pairs<br>• Doubling the final letter before adding *-ing* or *-ed*<br>• Alphabetical order | • Capital letters<br>• Comma<br>• Full stop |
| | | *Test 1* | |
| 4. Are There Paw-Prints in Heaven? | | • Simile | |
| 5. Sniffles the Crocodile and Punch the Butterfly | Factual, inferential and extrapolative | • Singular and plural nouns<br>• Compound words | • Question mark<br>• Exclamation mark<br>• Possessive pronouns<br>• Order of adjectives |
| 6. The Water Cycle | | • Suffixes | |
| | | *Test 2* | |
| 7. The Lantern and the Fan | Factual, inferential and extrapolative | • Words with *ie* and *ei* | • Simple present tense<br>• Present continuous tense |
| 8. A Letter to Grown-Ups | | • Finding environment-related words in the word grid<br>• Looking at picture clues and filling in the blanks | |
| 9. Peter Saves Wendy | Factual and inferential | • Opposites with prefixes *dis-* and *un-* | • Verb<br>• Simple past tense |
| | | *Test 3* | |
| 10. Marco Polo | Factual and inferential | • Identifying spelling errors and finding them in a word grid | • Prepositions of place<br>• Prepositions of movement<br>• *Can, can't, must, mustn't* |
| 11. On the Water | | • Antonyms<br>• Filling in the blanks with picture clues | |
| 12. The Mouse Maiden | Factual and inferential | • Sound words | • Conjunctions<br>• Adverbs, and adverbs of manner |
| 13. The Selfish Giant | Factual, inferential and extrapolative | • Synonyms<br>• Anagrams | • *Do/Does/Did* |
| | | *Test 4* | |

| | Listening and Speaking | Writing | Activity |
|---|---|---|---|
| | | | • Unscrambling words to answer riddles |
| | • Listening to information being read out and filling in the blanks<br>• Speaking about what one wants to be as a grown-up | • Picture storyboard: Completing a story | |
| | • Listening to a short story and sequencing<br>• Interviewing one's parents | • Writing an invitation | |
| | | | |
| | | | • Crafting birds with cardboard cut-outs |
| | • Listening to a short paragraph and marking T/F<br>• Discussing one's favourite bird or animal | • Writing a ten-line paragraph on one's pet | |
| | | | • Finding words related to water in the word grid |
| | | | |
| | • Listening to a passage and filling in the blanks<br>• /*f*/ sound in words with /*ph*/ and /*gh*/<br>• Reading words with the correct spelling<br>• Expressing agreement and disagreement in conversation | • Filling in the blanks to complete an informal letter | |
| | | | • Writing rhyming words for the names of ordinary things |
| | • Listening to a telephonic conversation and answering questions<br>• Giving instructions | • Describing an incident | |
| | | | |
| | • Listening to instructions and filling in the blanks<br>• Listening to *-ance* and *-ence* words and repeating them<br>• Talking about imaginary travel experiences | • Writing a list of solutions for a situation | |
| | | | • Drawing from memory of one's last vacation |
| | • Listening to a passage and filling in the blanks<br>• Reading homographs loudly to listen to pronunciation differences<br>• Listening to words with the long *oo* sound and repeating them | • Writing an informal letter | |
| | • Listening to a paragraph and sequencing<br>• Seeking permission in a role-play | • Filling in the blanks to complete a dialogue<br>• Making a list of character similarities and differences | |
| | | | |

# Contents

# 1 Limericks

## VOCABULARY

**A. Fill in the crossword. Use the clues to guess the words.**

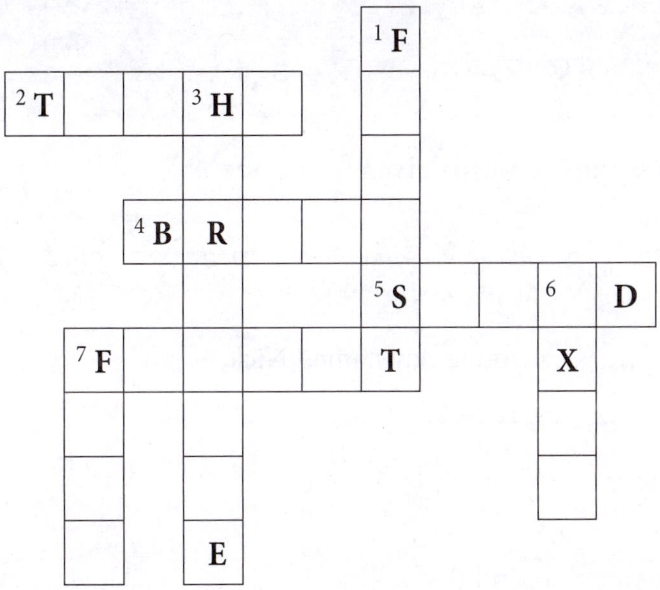


**Across**

2. I mean *closed firmly*, or *not loose*. I rhyme with *might*.
4. I mean *courageous*. I rhyme with *cave*.
5. I mean *a horse used to ride on*. I rhyme with *feed*.
7. I mean *a feeling of fear*. I rhyme with *write*.

**Down**

1. I mean *a large area of land thickly covered with trees*. I rhyme with *contest*.
3. I am another word for *unpleasant*. I rhyme with *adorable*.
6. I mean *a way out of a place*. I rhyme with *biscuit*.
7. I mean *the shape of something*. I rhyme with *storm*.

**B. Write three rhyming words for each word.**

1. blink .................................. .................................. ..................................
2. four .................................. .................................. ..................................
3. joy .................................. .................................. ..................................
4. melt .................................. .................................. ..................................
5. peace .................................. .................................. ..................................

## Limerick

- A **limerick** is a short funny poem containing five lines.
- The first two lines of a limerick are long, and they rhyme with each other. The next two lines are usually short, and they rhyme with each other. The fifth line is long, and it rhymes with the first two lines. For example:

*There was once a funny little* ***car,***
*Who wanted to turn into a* ***star.***
*It tried to fly with all its* ***might,***
*But it couldn't take* ***flight,***
*And fell to the ground without going* ***far.***

**C. Complete the limerick using the words given in the box.**

| *bright* | *jumped* | *cried* | *like* | *tried* | *once* |
|---|---|---|---|---|---|

There was .................................. a young boy named Nick,
Who a bully .................................. to kick.
Now, Nick did not .................................. to fight,
For he was kind and ...................................
So he .......................... to one side, and the bully .........................., 'How quick!'

**D. Write a poem with four or six lines on a topic of your choice. You may follow the example given below.**

*I had a dog named Custard.*
*It was always very flustered.*
*When I tried to take it out for a walk,*
*It would run and hide behind the big clock.*

..................................................................................................................................

..................................................................................................................................

 ..................................................................................................................................

..............................................................................................................................................

..............................................................................................................................................

..............................................................................................................................................

## ACTIVITY

**Unscramble the words in brackets to answer these riddles.**

1. I have silky white fur.
   I have a cartoon character named after me.
   I love carrots.
   Who am I?
   ........................................ (BATRBI)
2. I am yellowish-brown in colour.
   I carry my baby in my pouch.
   I don't walk, I hop.
   Who am I?
   ........................................ (GROAKNOA)
3. I am found in China.
   Bamboo shoots are my favourite food.
   I am very cute.
   Who am I?
   ........................................ (NPDAA)
4. I am a relative of the tiger and the lion.
   I am the fastest animal on land.
   I am covered with black spots.
   Who am I?
   ........................................ (HATECEH)
5. I am the ship of the desert.
   I can live without drinking water for several days.
   I have a hump on my back.
   Who am I?
   ........................................ (LECMA)

# 2 Birbal Identifies the Thief

## READING

**Read the passage and answer the questions.**

One day, a merchant bought a sack of salt at the market, and loaded it on his donkey. On their way home, they had to cross a stream. Accidentally, the donkey fell into the stream, and the salt melted in the water. The donkey was delighted because he did not have to carry a heavy load any more. The merchant returned to the market with his donkey and bought some more salt. On their way back, the donkey fell down at the same spot again, this time on purpose! He brayed in happiness because his load had become lighter.

The merchant understood the donkey's trick. He returned to the market once more, and bought a sack of sponge. When the donkey fell into the stream again, the sponge soaked up water and became heavier. Now, the donkey had to carry a much heavier load. He had learnt a lesson.

## COMPREHENSION

**A. Choose the correct option.**

1. The merchant first bought
   a. a sack of salt.
   b. a sack of sugar.
   c. a sack of flour.
2. While returning home, the merchant and his donkey had to cross
   a. a road.
   b. a bridge.
   c. a stream.

3. The third time, the merchant bought a sack of
   a. sugar.
   b. coal.
   c. sponge.
4. The second time, the donkey fell into the water
   a. by accident.
   b. because of weakness.
   c. on purpose.

**B. Answer the questions.**

1. How did the donkey fall down the first time?

   ..........

   ..........

2. What happened to the salt when the sack of salt fell into the stream?

   ..........

   ..........

3. Do you think the donkey would have continued falling into the stream if the merchant had not taught him a lesson? Give a reason for your answer.

   ..........

   ..........

4. Write the plurals of these words.

   a. donkey .......... b. sack ..........

## VOCABULARY

### Singular and Plural

- Nouns can be either **singular** or **plural.**
- **Singular** means *one.*
- **Plural** means *more than one.*

### Rules for forming plural forms

- For most nouns, we add *-s* to form the plural form. For example:

  *bottle – bottle**s***

  *pencil – pencil**s***

- When nouns end with a consonant before an *o*, we add *-es*. We also add *-es* when nouns end in *-ch, -x, -s, -sh,* or *-ss*. For example:

  | | | |
  |---|---|---|
  | *potato – potato**es*** | *box – box**es*** | *dish – dish**es*** |
  | *pouch – pouch**es*** | *bus – bus**es*** | *dress – dress**es*** |

- When nouns end in *-f* or *-fe*, we usually change them to *-v* and add *-es*. For example:

  *wolf – wolves*

  *wife – wives*

**A. Fill in the blanks with the correct plural form of the words in brackets.**

1. The ..................................... (*boy*) are happy because they have got new ..................................... (*bicycle*).
2. My mother bought some ..................................... (*mango*) for me.
3. I packed my ..................................... (*scarf*) in a bag.
4. I bought some fresh ..................................... (*loaf*) of bread.
5. Our captain won all the ..................................... (*toss*) in the tournament.
6. ..................................... (*leaf*) fall from trees in autumn.

**B. Write the singular form of each underlined word.**

| Singular | Plural |
|---|---|
| 1. ..................................... | a pack of <u>wolves</u> |
| 2. ..................................... | three <u>foxes</u> |
| 3. ..................................... | a basket of <u>tomatoes</u> |
| 4. ..................................... | half a dozen <u>books</u> |
| 5. ..................................... | a dozen <u>toothbrushes</u> |
| 6. ..................................... | some harmful <u>gases</u> |

## Countable and Uncountable nouns

- Nouns can be of two types—**countable** and **uncountable**.
- **Countable nouns** refer to things we can count. They have a singular and a plural form. For example:

  *one **cat** – two **cats***

  *one **shop** – many **shops***

- **Uncountable nouns** stand for things we cannot count. They may be the names of ideas, feelings, qualities, or other uncountable things. They usually do not have a plural form. For example:

  *happiness*    *wisdom*    *air*    *sugar*

**C. Use *a, an, some,* or *any* to fill in each blank.**

1. I had ..................... egg, ..................... glass of milk, and ..................... orange for breakfast.
2. Can you lend me ..................... money, please?

3. There isn't ...................... tea left in the teapot.
4. Please give me ...................... pencil to write with.
5. Can I have ...................... more pudding, please? I am sorry, there isn't ...................... left.
6. Would you like ...................... coffee?

**D. Underline the nouns in these sentences. Then write them down in the correct boxes.**

1. A boy fell down while crossing the bridge.
2. The weather in the hills is cold.
3. I like juice more than milk.
4. The ice cubes have melted into water.
5. The girl asked me for some money.
6. I gave her twenty rupees.

**Countable Nouns**

**Uncountable Nouns**

## GRAMMAR

### Common and Proper nouns

**Nouns** are names of any person, place, or thing.

#### Common nouns

**Common nouns** refer to people, places, animals, or things in general. They do not begin with a capital letter. For example:

*boy* *house* *dog* *flower*

## Proper nouns

**Proper nouns** refer to specific people, places, or other special names such as names of languages, companies, or brands. All proper nouns begin with a capital letter. For example:

*Priya* *New Delhi* *Qutab Minar* *French*

**A. Match these parts of sentences to make complete sentences.**

| Column A | Column B |
|---|---|
| 1. Vikramaditya was | a. in a Nike store. |
| 2. New Delhi is | b. read German? |
| 3. He works | c. are for my brother. |
| 4. These apples | d. a wise king. |
| 5. Can you | e. the capital of India. |

**B. Write the sentences you formed in the above exercise. Underline common nouns and circle proper nouns.**

1. ..........
2. ..........
3. ..........
4. ..........
5. ..........

## Collective nouns

A **collective noun** is the name used for a group of people, animals, or things. For example:

*Everyone in the* ***audience*** *laughed.*

*The* ***council*** *of ministers visited the accident site.*

*A* ***herd*** *of elephants walked through the forest.*

*A* ***flock*** *of birds flew over his head.*

**C. Fill in the blanks with the correct collective nouns from brackets.**

1. a .................................. (*flock*/*colony*) of ants

2. a .................................... (*brood*/*herd*) of chicks

3. a .................................... (*board*/*pack*) of dogs

4. a .................................... (*brood*/*caravan*) of camels

5. a .................................... (*pride*/*flock*) of lions

6. a .................................... (*council*/*troop*) of monkeys

**D. Match these common nouns with their correct collective nouns.**

| Common noun | Collective noun |
|---|---|
| 1. flowers | a. crew |
| 2. cattle | b. gaggle |
| 3. sailors | c. bouquet |
| 4. puppies | d. herd |
| 5. geese | e. litter |

**E. Write the words you matched in the previous exercise. One has been done for you.**

1. *a bouquet of flowers*
2. ..........................................................................
3. ..........................................................................
4. ..........................................................................
5. ..........................................................................

## LISTENING AND SPEAKING

### Listening

**A. Read through the information given to you. Now, listen to the teacher as she reads out the information. Fill in the blanks with the correct words from brackets.**

1. a. I travel by .............................. (*spacecraft/airplane/cruiser*).
   b. I wear a spacesuit with a big .............................. (*helmet/hat/cap*) on my head.
   c. I have visited the .............................. (*moon/sky/sun*).
   Who am I? ..............................
2. a. I love .............................. (*drum/sports/plays*) and movies.
   b. I play different ..............................(*roles/sores/shores*).
   c. I have to learn a lot of ..............................(*dialogues/tricks/trees*).
   Who am I? ..............................
3. a. I am always invited for weddings and .............................. (*movies/celebrations/school*).
   b. I can make copies in .............................. (*orange/blue/colour*) or black and white.
   c. I shoot people with my .............................. (*gun/pipe/camera*).
   Who am I? ..............................
4. a. I am the head cook in restaurants and .............................. (*plates/hotels/glasses*).
   b. I wear a starched .............................. (*bite/white/fight*) cap on my head.
   c. I make sure that .............................. (*customers/birds/waiters*) enjoy tasty dishes.
   Who am I? ..............................

### Speaking

**B. Look at the professions mentioned in the listening exercise given above. Do you wish to be one of them? Speak about what you want to be when you grow up. Give at least two reasons why.**

## WRITING

**Look at these pictures. Read the clue words and phrases provided. Write about Kevin's family in complete sentences. One has been done for you.**

**Kevin:** 7 years; studying in class 3; hobbies: cricket and painting; loves his family

**Mr Peter:** Kevin's grandfather; tall and balding; famous lawyer; plays cricket with Kevin

**Mrs Mary Peter:** Kevin's grandmother; excellent cook; bakes cakes; tells wonderful stories

*Hi! I am Kevin, and I am 7 years old. I am studying in class 3. My favourite hobbies are playing cricket and painting. I love my grandparents very much. Let me tell you about them.*

*My grandfather's name is* ..............................................................................

# 3 Think Hard, Boatman

## READING

**Read the poem and answer the questions.**

**Ferry Me Across the Water**

'Ferry me across the water,
Do, boatman, do.'

'If you've a penny in your purse
I'll ferry you.'

'I have a penny in my purse,
And my eyes are blue;
So ferry me across the water,
Do, boatman, do.'

'Step into my ferry-boat,
Be they black or blue,
And for the penny in your purse
I'll ferry you.'

–*Christina Rossetti*

## COMPREHENSION

**A. Choose the correct option.**

1. Who is the poet talking to?
   a. the coachman
   b. the boatman
   c. the fisherman

2. Where does the poet want to go?
   a. over the hill
   b. across the water
   c. under the bridge
3. Does the boatman agree to take the poet on his ferry?
   a. yes
   b. no
   c. the poem doesn't mention
4. What colour are the poet's eyes?
   a. blue
   b. green
   c. black

**B. Read the lines from the poem and answer the questions.**

1. *'I have a penny in my purse,*
   *And my eyes are blue;*
   *So ferry me across the water,*
   *Do, boatman, do.'*

   a. Why does the poet tell the boatman that she has a penny?

   ........................................................................................................

   ........................................................................................................

   b. What does the poet mean by *ferry me*?

   ........................................................................................................

   ........................................................................................................

2. *'Step into my ferry-boat,*
   *Be they black or blue,*
   *And for the penny in your purse*
   *I'll ferry you.'*

   a. What is *they* here?

   ........................................................................................................

   ........................................................................................................

   b. Do you think it matters to the boatman if the poet's eyes are blue? Give a reason for your answer.

   ........................................................................................................

   ........................................................................................................

**C. Write the words that rhyme with *blue* in the poem.**

1. ..............................................................

2. ..............................................................

# VOCABULARY

## Word pairs

Some words are used in pairs, and always appear in an agreed order. For example:

*black and white* (*not* white and black)

*hot and cold* (*not* cold and hot)

**A. Complete these word pairs.**

1. lock and ....................
2. hide and ....................
3. high and ....................
4. day and ....................
5. forgive and ....................
6. backwards and ....................

## Spelling

### Doubling the final letter before adding *-ing* or *-ed*

When a one-syllable word ends with a vowel followed by a consonant, we double the last letter (the consonant) before adding *-ing* or *-ed*. For example:

| | | |
|---|---|---|
| ref**er** | refe**rr**ing | refe**rr**ed |
| st**op** | sto**pp**ing | sto**pp**ed |
| dr**ip** | dri**pp**ing | dri**pp**ed |

**B. Write the correct *-ing* and *-ed* forms of these words.**

1. beg .................... ....................
2. slip .................... ....................
3. grab .................... ....................
4. hop .................... ....................
5. hug .................... ....................
6. tag .................... ....................

# DICTIONARY SKILLS

## Alphabetical order

- A dictionary is a book that lists all the words of a language. It also gives their meanings.
- All the words in a dictionary are listed in **alphabetical order**. It makes the word search easier and quicker.
- The following words are in alphabetical order. Look at the first letter of every word:

  *carrot* *forest* *happy* *jacket* *powder*

  **C**, of *carrot*, is the third letter of the alphabet.

  **F**, of *forest*, is the sixth letter.

  **H**, of *happy*, is the eighth letter.

  **J**, of *jacket*, is the tenth letter.

  **P**, of *powder*, is the sixteenth letter.

**Place the following months of the year in alphabetical order.**

| | | | |
|---|---|---|---|
| January | November | August | February |
| September | December | July | |

# GRAMMAR

## Capital letter

- A sentence always begins with a capital letter. For example:

  *My name is Ashish.*

  *The army protects us from our enemies.*

- Proper nouns begin with a capital letter. For example:

  ***I**ndia* ***J**awaharlal **N**ehru* ***T**aj **M**ahal* ***S**unday*

**A. Rewrite these sentences using capital letters wherever necessary.**

1. we are going to america in december.

   ..............................................................................................................................

2. i baked a cake for christmas.

   ..............................................................................................................................

3. hyderabad is the capital of telangana.

   ..............................................................................................................................

4. ravi is starting his new session on monday.

   ..............................................................................................................................

5. rehman is an obedient child.

   ..............................................................................................................................

## Comma

A **comma** (,) is used to separate words in a list. For example:

*I like writing stories, poems, letters, and essays.*

*The four seasons in a year are spring, summer, autumn, and winter.*

## Full stop

A **full stop** (.) is used at the end of a sentence. It shows that the sentence is complete. For example:

*The principal did not come to school today.*

*Grandfather was happy at his birthday party.*

**B. Read these sentences. Insert commas wherever necessary.**

1. Papa bought a refrigerator a washing machine an air conditioner and a microwave oven.
2. My four dogs are named Rover Timmy Skipper and Flash.
3. I enjoy swimming running cycling and skipping rope.
4. Tara made a cake using a cup of flour some sugar a bottle of milk a chocolate and a few berries.
5. Suraj put three pencils two erasers a box of crayons and some notebooks on his desk.

**C. Rewrite these sentences using capital letters, commas, and full stops wherever necessary.**

1. the atacama desert is in south america

   ..........................................................................................

2. tom hari rehman and rajesh are good friends

   ..........................................................................................

3. he is hard-working skillful polite and kind

   ..........................................................................................

4. i can speak english spanish italian and french

   ..........................................................................................

5. new delhi is the capital of india

   ..........................................................................................

6. the first five months of a year are january february march april and may

   ..........................................................................................

## LISTENING AND SPEAKING

### Listening

**A. Listen to a short story. Put the sentences in the correct order. One has been done for you.**

- The tortoise won the race. ☐
- The hare went to sleep. ☐
- The hare was proud of its speed and ran very fast. ☐
- The hare saw the tortoise was far behind. ☐
- The tortoise walked slowly but steadily. ☐
- Once a hare and a tortoise had a race. [1]

### Speaking

**B. Interview your parents about what they do at their respective workplaces. You may ask questions like these:**

- *Where do you work?*
- *What do you do?*
- *Do you love what you do?*

## WRITING

**Your school is organising a dance festival for your class. Write an invitation inviting all the parents to attend this event.**

**Do not forget to mention the venue, date, time, and a short description of the event in the space given on the next page.**

Date: ..........................................

Time: ..........................................

Venue: ..........................................

Title of the event: ..........................................

Description of the event:

..........................................

..........................................

..........................................

..........................................

..........................................

..........................................

..........................................

..........................................

..........................................

..........................................

..........................................

..........................................

..........................................

..........................................

Regards,

..........................................

(Your name)

# TEST 1

## VOCABULARY ............................................................................................................(5)

**A. Make plurals of these nouns by adding *s* or *es*:** **(2)**

1. mango ..................................................
2. ant ..................................................
3. nest ..................................................
4. watch ..................................................

**B. Read the instructions. Then, rewrite the words correctly.** **(1)**

1. dip (add *-ed*) : ..................................................
2. begin (add *-ing*) : ..................................................

**C. Match the words in the two columns to form word pairs:** **(2)**

| Column A | Column B |
|---|---|
| 1. odds and | a. downs |
| 2. top and | b. ends |
| 3. ups and | c. found |
| 4. lost and | d. bottom |

## GRAMMAR ............................................................................................................(10)

**A. There are two common nouns and two proper nouns in this passage. Underline the nouns. Then, write the nouns under the given columns.** **(4)**

I have a dog. I love my dog very much. I call it Pixie. I have a cat too. It is called Kitty. It is very playful.

| Common nouns | Proper nouns |
|---|---|
| | |
| | |

**B. Fill in each blank with the correct word from the box. Be careful! There are two extra words.** **(4)**

| *bundle* | *grove* | *pack* | *box* | *flight* | *range* |
|---|---|---|---|---|---|

1. A ............................................ of mountains
2. A ............................................ of clothes
3. A ............................................ of cards
4. A ............................................ of trees

**C. Rewrite the following sentences using capital letters, full stop or commas wherever necessary:** **(2)**

a. India is a beautiful country

........................................................................................................................................

b. Ravi and rohit have a dog a cat a horse a goat and a donkey in their farm

........................................................................................................................................

# 4 Are There Paw-prints in Heaven?

## VOCABULARY

### Simile

A **simile** is used to compare two different things by using the word *as* or *like*. For example:

*Priya is* ***as*** *brave* ***as*** *a lion.*

*My grandfather eats* ***like*** *a bird.*

**Read these sentences. Fill in the blanks using similes for the words in brackets. One has been done for you.**

1. The night was ....as black as coal.... (*black/coal*).
2. In the distance, there was something shining .................................................. (*bright/a diamond*).
3. I ran towards the light .................................................. (*fast/a cheetah*).
4. I reached a lake. The water was .................................................. (*clear/glass*).
5. A woman stood next to it. She was .................................................. (*tall/a tree*).
6. She looked .................................................. (*proud/a peacock*).
7. Later, I came to know she was .................................................. (*gentle/a lamb*).
8. She pointed a finger towards the sky. A shooting star travelled through the sky .................................................. (*quick/lightning*).
9. Far in the distance, I saw the moon. It was .................................................. (*round/a coin*).
10. On the Annual Sports Day, Nithya ran .................................................. (*fast/the wind*).
11. Raghu was amazed to see the dancer move .................................................. (*gracefully/a deer*).
12. On top of the hill, there stood an oak tree .................................................. (*old/time*).

## Bird craft

**Let's make a bird craft.**

**Materials required:**

- Cardboard cut-outs of different birds
- Some fallen twigs
- Glue
- Chart paper

**Steps:**

1. Paste twigs on the chart paper with the help of glue. Let it dry for a while.
2. Now, paste the cut-outs of different birds on the twigs so that they look like birds sitting on branches. Let it dry for a while.

**Your bird craft is ready. Bring it to class and share it with your classmates. Identify and name the birds in their bird craft.**

# 5 Sniffles the Crocodile and Punch the Butterfly

## READING

**Read the passage and answer the questions.**

The Bengal tiger is the national animal of India. It is light or dark orange in colour, with black stripes on its skin. It has yellow eyes. It has a lot of strength and energy, and can swim and even climb trees.

Tigers are nocturnal animals, which means that they sleep during the day, and hunt for food at night. Tigers are found in many states in India, and in neighbouring countries like Nepal, Bhutan, and Bangladesh. They live in thick jungles, mangrove swamps, and tall grasslands.

F.— Tigris. Tiger.

*Project Tiger* is a tiger conservation programme that protects tigers from extinction. As on 30 October, 2017, the project has set up 50 tiger reserves in India.

## COMPREHENSION

**A. Choose the correct option.**

1. Which is the national animal of India?
   - a. the tiger
   - b. the lion
   - c. the peacock

2. What is the colour of the stripes on the tiger's skin?
   a. red
   b. orange
   c. black
3. Where do tigers live?
   a. in the sea
   b. in thick jungles
   c. in a nest
4. According to the passage, how many tiger reserves are there in India?
   a. 21
   b. 50
   c. 45
5. Which of these sentences is true?
   a. Tigers can swim and climb trees.
   b. Tigers sleep during the day, and hunt for food at night.
   c. Both a. and b.

**B. Answer the questions.**

1. Write two sentences on the national animal of India.

   ..........................................................................................

   ..........................................................................................

2. What is *Project Tiger*?

   ..........................................................................................

   ..........................................................................................

3. Why do you think it is important to set up tiger reserves? Give a reason for your answer.

   ..........................................................................................

   ..........................................................................................

4. Write the plural forms of these words.
   a. animal ..............................
   b. country ..............................

## VOCABULARY

### Singular and Plural nouns

- **Singular** means *one*. For example:

  *boat* *tree* *lion* *jungle*

- **Plural** means *more than one.*

- For most nouns, we add *-s* at the end of the word to make a plural word. For example:

  *boats* *trees* *lions* *jungles*

- For nouns that end with *-ch*, *-x*, *-s*, *-sh*, or *-ss*, we add *-es*. For example:

  *switch* → *switches* *fox* → *foxes* *gas* → *gases* *wish* → *wishes* *glass* → *glasses*

- For nouns that end with *-f* or *-fe*, we change them to a *-v*, and then add *-es*. For example:

  *leaf* → *leaves* *wife* → *wives*

- When the letter before the final *-y* is a consonant, change the *-y* to an *-i*, and then add *-es*. For example:

  *baby* → *babies* *army* → *armies* *diary* → *diaries*

- When the letter before a *-y* is a vowel, **do not** change the *-y*. Just add *-s* to make a plural. For example:

  *day* → *days* *donkey* → *donkeys* *toy* → *toys*

**A. Fill in the blanks with the correct singular and plural words. One has been done for you.**

1. I live in a joint *family*, with my grandparents and cousins.

Many small *families* live in a block of flats.

2. This is a pink ..............................

Oh! What a beautiful bunch of ..............................

3. Our housetop has a red ..............................

The ................................ in my area emit a lot of smoke.

4. The child's ................................ was heard by the mother.

The sad ................................ of the children could be heard from a long distance.

**B. Choose the correct singular or plural noun and fill in the blanks. One has been done for you.**

1. We became afraid when we heard the loud howl of a wolf (*wolf/wolves*).
2. The tree outside our house has many ................................ (*branch/branches*).
3. She has long black ................................ (*eyelash/eyelashes*).
4. I had only one English ................................ (*class/classes*) today.
5. A ................................ (*thief/thieves*) was caught near our house last night.

## Compound words

**Compound words** are words that are formed by combining two smaller words. For example:

*jelly + fish = jellyfish*    *cup + cake = cupcake*

**C. Make compound words by combining the most suitable word from each set with the first word of that set.**

| | | | | | |
|---|---|---|---|---|---|
| 1. table: | wood | cloth | spoon | vase | ................................ |
| 2. earth: | quake | tree | leaf | worm | ................................ |
| 3. door: | bell | stand | window | glass | ................................ |
| 4. note: | rupee | pen | book | white | ................................ |
| 5. hair: | wool | comb | cut | time | ................................ |

# GRAMMAR

## Question mark

A **question mark** (?) is used to show that a question has been asked. It is placed at the end of a sentence. For example:

*Where is the kite you were flying just now?*

*Who is visiting us this evening?*

## Exclamation mark

An **exclamation mark** (!) shows a strong feeling like excitement, anger, or surprise. It is usually placed at the end of a sentence or after interjections. Interjections are words that are used to express anger or surprise. For example:

*Stop behaving like that!*

*Wow! It's a lovely car.*

**A. Read these sentences. Insert question marks and exclamation marks wherever necessary.**

1. What a lovely view
2. I am so upset with you
3. How was your annual function last night
4. Did you talk to Sameer about the trip
5. Put it down
6. Why did you come home late

## Possessive pronouns

A **possessive pronoun** is a type of pronoun that shows ownership of something. For example:

*These four glasses are* ***mine****.*

*This house belongs to* ***her****.*

*This pen is* ***yours****.*

**B. Fill in the blanks with the correct possessive pronouns.**

1. That toy belongs to those children. That toy is .......................................
2. That bicycle belongs to me. That bicycle is .......................................
3. That footwear belongs to my mother. That footwear is .......................................
4. That book belongs to you. That book is .......................................
5. That laptop belongs to my father. That laptop is .......................................

## Order of adjectives

Words that describe nouns are called **adjectives**. Sometimes, more than one adjective is used to describe a noun. In such a case, the adjectives must appear in a *certain order*.

- At first place are adjectives that give the number of persons or things: ***two** houses.*
- At second place are adjectives that give the opinion about the noun: *two **lovely** houses.*
- At third place are adjectives that give the size, shape, age, or colour of the noun: *two lovely, **little, old, red** houses.*
- At fourth place are adjectives that give the nationality of the noun: *two lovely, little, old, red, **French** houses.*
- At fifth place are adjectives that give the material of the noun: *two lovely, little, old, red, French, **wooden** houses.*

**C. Place the adjectives given in brackets in the correct order.**

1. The ........................................ (*nice/old*) man was shivering.

2. I have ........................................ (*colourful/two*) kites.

3. There is a ........................................ (*tall/green*) tree in the park.

4. The sparrows built a ........................................ (*round/pretty*) nest.

5. I have a ........................................ (*green/long*) frock.

6. We live in a ........................................ (*large/wooden/brown*) house.

## LISTENING AND SPEAKING

### Listening

**A. Listen to a short paragraph. Then mark the sentences as true (T) or false (F).**

1. There were four friends who visited the zoo. ☐
2. Priya bought the tickets for all of them. ☐
3. They saw ducks and swans. ☐
4. The boys did not see the lions. ☐
5. The girls loved the colourful parrots. ☐

### Speaking

**B. What is your favourite bird or animal? Tell your friend what you like about it, where it lives or is generally found, where you saw it and what it looks like.**

## WRITING

**Write a ten-line paragraph about your pet. If you do not have a pet, imagine you have one. Write its name, what kind of animal it is, what its favourite food is, what games you play with it, and how you take care of it. Give your paragraph a title.**

# 6 The Water Cycle

## VOCABULARY

### Suffix

- A **suffix** is a letter or group of letters that are added to the end of a word to make a new and different word.
- Some common suffixes are: *-ly*, *-ness*, *-less*, *-ful*, *-ment*, *-able*, and *-al*.
  For example:

| | | | |
|---|---|---|---|
| *quick**ly*** | *sad**ness*** | *help**less*** | *sorrow**ful*** |
| *punish**ment*** | *present**able*** | *recit**al*** | |

- We can also use suffixes to make the opposites of some words. For example:

  *doubt**ful** – doubt**less***    *joy**ful** – joy**less***    *care**ful** – care**less***

**A. Write the opposites of these words by adding suitable suffixes.**

1. powerful ……………………
2. painless ……………………
3. fearless ……………………
4. harmful ……………………
5. hopeful ……………………
6. shameless ……………………

**B. Fill in the blanks with the correct suffixes from brackets.**

1. Sara's eager...................... (*-less*/*-ness*) to help her mother was liked by everyone.
2. Her exam results were remark...................... (*-able*/*-ment*).
3. The shopkeeper packed the gift nice...................... (*-ful*/*-ly*).
4. Ayaan couldn't hide his excite...................... (*-ment*/*-less*) before the football match.
5. The antics of Charlie Chaplin are so comic...................... (*-full*/*-al*).

## ACTIVITY

**The water words given below are hidden in the grid. Find them.**

| F | L | U | I | D | X | Y | G | V | L | R | L |
|---|---|---|---|---|---|---|---|---|---|---|---|
| A | L | M | W | U | R | E | L | C | Y | R | A |
| L | K | I | Y | W | A | X | I | I | D | E | K |
| C | E | O | D | A | I | C | Q | R | T | H | E |
| Q | R | G | W | T | N | M | U | I | S | O | M |
| E | B | O | C | E | A | N | I | V | J | Y | F |
| L | W | P | W | R | X | H | D | E | F | V | E |
| N | Z | O | J | F | S | Q | D | R | X | U | G |
| R | C | O | W | A | P | I | I | S | U | A | G |
| H | F | L | H | L | R | Q | D | N | C | A | K |
| I | C | E | Z | L | A | H | P | V | M | D | U |
| V | T | T | T | N | Y | F | K | P | B | T | Y |

1. FLUID 2. ICE 3. RIVER 4. RAIN 5. SPRAY
6. LAKE 7. WATERFALL 8. LIQUID 9. POOL 10. OCEAN

# TEST 2

## VOCABULARY ..................................................(5)

**A. Read the following sentences. Add a suitable suffix to the word given in brackets to fill in the blanks.** **(1)**

1. He does his work with care. He is a .............................................. (care) worker.
2. He is not afraid of anything. He is a .............................................. (fear) child.

**B. Fill in the blanks with the correct form of the nouns given in brackets.** **(1.5)**

1. There are many new .................................... (leaf) on the tree.
2. There are many .................................... (dish) to be washed.
3. Mumbai and Kolkata are crowded .................................... (city).

**C. Match the words with their suitable similes.** **(2.5)**

| Column A | Column B |
|---|---|
| 1. As old as | a. a cheetah |
| 2. As white as | b. a snail |
| 3. As slow as | c. an elephant |
| 4. As big as | d. the hills |
| 5. As fast as | e. snow |

## GRAMMAR ..................................................(10)

**A. Add '?' or '!' correctly at the end of each sentence.** **(4)**

1. What a beautiful painting
2. Did you buy this dress in Hyderabad
3. How hard it rains
4. How will father drive home in this rain

**B. Make a sentence with these words. Put the adjectives in the correct order.** **(4)**

1. red, silk, big umbrella

   ........................................................................................................................................

2. black, big, strong panther

   ........................................................................................................................................

3. short, cotton, blue dress

   ........................................................................................................................................

4. beautiful, Chinese, old vases

   ........................................................................................................................................

**C. Insert the correct possessive pronouns to complete sentences.** **(2)**

1. Mr and Mrs Verma own that red car. The car is ........................................
2. I gifted a book to Daisy. It is ........................................
3. I bought a new watch yesterday. This watch is ........................................
4. You have a red bottle. This red bottle is ........................................

# 7 The Lantern and the Fan

## READING

**Read the passage and answer the questions.**

Malala Yousafzai, a girl from Pakistan, won the Nobel Peace Prize in 2014. She was just 17 at that time, and became the youngest person to receive the prestigious award. Malala won the Nobel Prize for starting a peaceful movement to promote the education of women and children. When Malala was 15 years old, she was attacked and badly injured by a set of bad people. These people were against the education of women. They wanted to prevent her from bringing change against the education.

*Malala Yousafzai*

However, this only made Malala more courageous and confident. After having recovered from her injuries, she continued to work towards her goal. Soon, she started to get international recognition. On 12 July, 2013, Malala's 16th birthday, she delivered a speech at the United Nations in support of women education. Today, she has become an inspiration for millions of girls around the world.

## COMPREHENSION

**A. Choose the correct option.**

1. Malala is from
   a. India.
   b. the United Nations.
   c. Pakistan.
2. When Malala won the Nobel Peace Prize, she was
   a. 17 years old.
   b. 21 years old.
   c. 15 years old.

3. Malala started a movement
    a. for the education of women and children.
    b. to save animals.
    c. to promote a healthy lifestyle.
4. Malala was attacked by
    a. people who believed that all children should go to school.
    b. people who were against the education of women.
    c. people who were against the education of boys.
5. Malala delivered a speech on
    a. her first day of school.
    b. World Environment Day.
    c. her sixteenth birthday.

**B. Answer the questions.**

1. In which year did Malala win the Nobel Peace Prize?

    ..........................................................................................

    ..........................................................................................

2. How old was Malala when she was attacked?

    ..........................................................................................

    ..........................................................................................

3. Why is it important to provide proper education to every child? Give a reason for your answer.

    ..........................................................................................

    ..........................................................................................

4. Write two synonyms for each of these words.
    a. injure .............................. ..............................
    b. peaceful .............................. ..............................

## VOCABULARY

### Words with *ie* and *ei*

- Use ***i*** before ***e***, except after ***c***, when the sound is ***ee***. For example:

    *brief* (there is no ***c*** in the word, so we use ***ie***; it makes the sound ***ee***)

    *ceiling* (the ***c*** in this word comes before ***e*** and ***i***, so we use ***ei***; it makes the sound ***ee***)

- Sometimes, ***ei*** is also used in words that may not have a ***c*** before ***ei***. In these words, the sound made by ***ei*** is like the alphabet ***a***. For example:

    *neighbour*    *weight*

**Fill in the blanks with the correct spellings of the words given in brackets.**

1. The police have not yet caught the ................................ (*theif/thief*).
2. Have you ................................ (*received/recieved*) your report card yet?
3. Santa Claus rode in on a ................................ (*sleigh/sliegh*).
4. My ................................ (*neice/niece*) will visit me this summer.
5. It is unfair to ................................ (*decieve/deceive*) anyone.
6. The mysterious woman was wearing a ................................ (*viel/veil*).

# GRAMMAR

## Simple present tense

- The **simple present tense** is used when talking about something that is a fact at the present time. For example:

  *My elder brother is ten years old.*

  *I work in London.*

- It is also used when talking about habits, daily and repeated events, and feelings. For example:

  *She walks a hundred metres every day.*

  *The bus leaves at 7:00 a.m.*

- It is also used for giving instructions and directions. For example:

  *The show begins at 4:30 p.m.*

  *Take a right at the end of the street.*

- The simple present tense is also used to state universal truths or facts. For example:

  *The Earth circles the Sun.*

  *India is in Asia.*

### Adding -*s* or -*es*

Add -***s*** or -***es*** to verbs used in the simple present tense when talking about a person. For example:

*She* ***plays*** *the piano.*

*He* ***teaches*** *football to young children.*

**A. Fill in the blanks with the simple present tense form of the verbs in brackets.**

1. Arjun ...................... (*am/is*) short.
2. Jane ...................... (*drink/smell*) tea very often.
3. He ...................... (*watch/give*) his favourite show every Tuesday.

4. The metro ...................... (*start/clean*) at 6 every morning.
5. Babies ...................... (*are/is*) cute.
6. Students ...................... (*work/sleep*) very hard to score well in exams.

### Present continuous tense

- The **present continuous tense** is used to talk about actions and events that are going on at the time of talking.
- The present continuous tense forms are made by using ***is***, ***am***, or ***are***, followed by the ***verb*** + ***-ing***. For example:

  *She **is** eat**ing**.*

  *I **am** sleep**ing**.*

  *We **are** go**ing** home.*

**B. Fill in the blanks with the correct present continuous form of the verbs given in brackets. One has been done for you.**

1. They ......are playing...... (*play*) a football match.
2. Sheela ................................ (*do*) her homework.
3. I ................................ (*study*) to become a vet.
4. We ................................ (*work*) on a puzzle.
5. Raheem ................................ (*feed*) the cat.
6. I ................................ (*build*) a sandcastle.
7. They ................................ (*wait*) for the bus.

## LISTENING AND SPEAKING

### Listening

**A. Listen to a passage and fill in the blanks. Make sure you spell the words correctly.**

1. The India Gate monument is located in ..........................................
2. The .......................................... passes by this monument every year.
3. It was built in the memory of thousands of .......................................... who fought in the ..........................................
4. India Gate is a very popular .......................................... destination.
5. The monument is .......................................... tall.

## Pronunciation

- The letters ***ph*** sound like the letter ***/f/***. For example:

    *graph* *sphere*

- Sometimes, the letters ***gh*** also sound like the letter ***/f/***. For example:

    *cough* *rough*

## Speaking

**B. Some of the words in these sentences are spelt incorrectly. Write the correct spelling above the misspelt word and read it aloud. One has been done for you.**

laughter

1. They say that laufter is the best medicine.
2. I asked my father to take a foto of me riding an elefant.
3. Did you get Ranbir's autograf?
4. The poor orfan was treated badly.
5. The milk is not enuff for all of us.
6. Did you watch the dolfin show yesterday?

**C. Talk to your friend about what is more important in general—reading or playing? Use expressions and phrases to agree and disagree in a conversation.**

# WRITING

**After reading the story of *The Lantern and the Fan*, you plan to write a letter to your friend telling him/her about the story. Fill in the blanks with the correct form of the words given in brackets to complete the letter.**

Dear .................................................. (write the name of your friend here)

Today we .................................. (*read*) the story of *The Lantern and the Fan* in class. I was very .................................. (*impress*) and .................................. (*delight*) by this story. I was taken aback when the father-in-law .................................. (*give*) the task to the two wives. They must have been so .................................. (*scare*) when they couldn't solve the riddles. I can only imagine the joy they .................................. (*feel*) when the voice in the forest .................................. (*help*) them.

The story of origami and invention inspired me. I hope to invent something someday.

Your loving friend

.................................................. (write your name)

# 8 A Letter to Grown-Ups

## VOCABULARY

**A. Find the given environment-related words in the grid.**

**Hint: Some of them may be upside down.**

| M | W | U | R | C | C | G | V | X | N | W | W | B | B | R |
|---|---|---|---|---|---|---|---|---|---|---|---|---|---|---|
| P | Z | M | B | L | I | L | E | R | O | Y | N | H | N | E |
| B | I | O | D | I | V | E | R | S | I | T | Y | V | M | N |
| T | T | N | H | M | N | Q | P | C | T | W | P | N | J | E |
| X | H | P | C | A | R | G | O | O | U | D | B | C | T | W |
| U | G | D | E | T | O | N | U | U | L | G | F | E | L | A |
| G | U | X | J | E | K | F | G | Y | L | G | H | D | I | B |
| T | O | R | U | D | Z | Z | E | N | O | C | J | I | O | L |
| T | R | P | B | W | W | Y | Y | Y | P | I | N | T | S | E |
| E | D | B | C | W | F | G | Q | N | L | Q | H | I | R | N |
| O | X | Y | G | E | N | O | O | C | F | E | H | G | N | L |
| B | T | L | W | B | V | L | U | E | E | V | J | W | A | U |
| C | G | Z | Z | H | Q | O | T | R | T | F | C | J | O | L |
| A | H | G | S | B | N | C | A | H | T | X | Z | G | B | R |
| M | O | P | R | E | S | E | R | V | A | T | I | O | N | S |

1. ECOLOGY 2. DROUGHT 3. POLLUTION 4. TIDE 5. PRESERVATION
6. RENEWABLE 7. SOIL 8. OXYGEN 9. CLIMATE 10. BIODIVERSITY

**B. Look at these pictures. Write the words or phrases that come to your mind while looking at them. One has been done for you.**

1. *electricity*
   *switch*
   *turn the light off*
   *turn the fan off*
   *save energy*

2. ..............................
   ..............................
   ..............................
   ..............................

3. ..............................
   ..............................
   ..............................
   ..............................
   ..............................

4. ..............................
   ..............................
   ..............................
   ..............................
   ..............................

## ACTIVITY

**Make a list of five things found in your room and five things found in your kitchen. Now write a rhyming word for each of them. One has been done for you.**

**Your room:**

1. chair ............ care
2. ............ ............
3. ............ ............
4. ............ ............
5. ............ ............

**Your kitchen:**

1. ............ ............
2. ............ ............
3. ............ ............
4. ............ ............
5. ............ ............

# 9 Peter Saves Wendy

## READING

**Read this passage about a girl named Dorothy and her dog, Toto, who set out to meet a great wizard. On their way, they meet a Scarecrow.**

Dorothy picked up her basket. 'Come along, Toto,' she said. 'We will go to the Emerald City and meet the Great Oz.' And so, with Toto trotting behind her, she started on her journey, her silver shoes tinkling merrily on the yellow-brick road. There were neat fences at the sides of the road, and beyond them were fields of grain and vegetables.

When she had gone several miles she thought she would stop to rest, and so climbed to the top of the fence and sat down. Not far away she saw a Scarecrow, placed high on a pole to keep the birds from the ripe corn. Its head was a small sack stuffed with straw, with eyes, nose, and mouth painted on it to represent a face. She was surprised to see one of the eyes slowly wink at her. The figure nodded its head to her in a friendly way.

*(An abridged extract from L. Frank Baum's The Wizard of Oz)*

## COMPREHENSION

**A. Choose the correct option.**

1. Dorothy was on her way to which city?
   a. Paris
   b. London
   c. Emerald City

2. Who was Dorothy travelling with?
   a. Her dog, Toto.
   b. An elephant named, Pronto.
   c. She was travelling alone.
3. What was the colour of the road Dorothy was walking on?
   a. black
   b. yellow
   c. can't say
4. What was on the sides of the road?
   a. fences
   b. lakes
   c. markets

**B. Answer the questions.**

1. What did the fields grow?

   ..........................................................................................

   ..........................................................................................

2. Why did Dorothy decide to sit down?

   ..........................................................................................

   ..........................................................................................

3. What did she see in the distance? What did it look like?

   ..........................................................................................

   ..........................................................................................

4. What did the Scarecrow do when Dorothy saw him? Why do you think she was surprised?

   ..........................................................................................

   ..........................................................................................

5. Write the opposites of these words.

   a. far ........................ c. neat ........................
   b. high ........................ d. friendly ........................

## VOCABULARY

### Prefix

- A **prefix** is a letter or group of letters that are added to the beginning of a word to make a new word.
- Prefixes like ***dis***- and ***un***- can be used to make the opposites of some words. For example:

  *honest – **dis**honest* *related – **un**related*

**Use *dis-* or *un-* with the words in brackets to fill in the blanks.**

1. The cat ran down the street and .................................... (*appeared*) quickly.
2. She was .................................... (*able*) to complete the test.
3. I am going to .................................... (*connect*) those wires.
4. Ram .................................... (*agreed*) with his friend.
5. Fast foods are .................................... (*healthy*).
6. The umpire's decision was .................................... (*fair*).

## GRAMMAR

### Verbs

A **verb** is a word that is used to describe an action. For example:

*The teacher **read** us a story from the* Panchatantra.

*She **closes** the door and **walks** to her car.*

**A. Look at the pictures and fill in the blanks with suitable verbs. One has been done for you.**

1. The boy ....*hit*.... the ball with his bat.

2. The little girl .............................. the rope.

3. The lady .............................. dinner.

4. The gardener .............................. the flowers.

5. Joe .................................. his book.

6. The girl .................................. her bicycle.

## Simple past tense

- The **simple past tense** of a verb shows the actions that happened some time ago (in the past) or the things that existed before the present time. For example:

  *Anna* ***entered*** *the classroom after me.*

  *Rome was* ***ruled*** *by mighty kings.*

- Regular verbs can be turned into simple past tense verbs by adding ***-d***, ***-ed***, or ***-ied*** to the end of the base form of the verb. For example:

  *The shop clos**ed** its doors.*

  *It rain**ed** in the morning.*

  *The paint dr**ied** yesterday.*

- The simple past tenses of the verb ***to be*** are **was** and **were**. For example:

  *She* ***was*** *here.*

  *The trains* ***were*** *late.*

**B. Fill in the blanks with the past form of the verbs given in brackets. One has been done for you.**

1. She ......tried...... (*try*) running faster than her dog.
2. They were .................................. (*marry*) in a church.
3. Tina .................................. (*visit*) a lot of interesting places.
4. It .................................. (*be*) fantastic.
5. It was a sad situation, but Mohit .................................. (*laugh*) instead.
6. My grandmother .................................. (*arrive*) last night.
7. The bags .................................. (*be*) very heavy.

## LISTENING AND SPEAKING

### Listening

**A. Sanaya's best friend, Sam, called. Since Sanaya was not at home, her sister answered the telephone. Listen to the conversation between Sanaya's sister and Sam. Then mark these sentences as true (T) or false (F).**

1. Sanaya was at home when Sam called. ☐
2. Sam and Sanaya are in the same piano class. ☐
3. Sanaya had gone to the market with her cousin. ☐
4. Sanaya's sister didn't know when Sanaya would come back. ☐
5. Sam left a message for Sanaya about their Monday class. ☐
6. Sanaya's sister didn't say goodbye to Sam. ☐

### Speaking

**B. Imagine you have to place an order at the grocery store. Instruct them to deliver a loaf of bread, a dozen eggs, a carton of milk, two packets of almond biscuits, and six oranges to your house. Role-play with your parent or a friend. Do not forget to mention the delivery address and the time of delivery.**

## WRITING

**Imagine you saw a man save a drowning child. Use the clue phrases in the box to describe the incident. Give a suitable title to your paragraph.**

*child stood near the edge of the river bank*    *the child fell into the river*    *a crowd gathered*
*some people called for help*    *one man came to the rescue of the drowning child*
*jumped into the river*    *saved the child*    *everyone praised him*

..............................................................

..............................................................................................................................................................

..............................................................................................................................................................

..............................................................................................................................................................

# TEST 3

## VOCABULARY ........................................................................................................(5)

**A. Fill in the blanks with *ei* or *ie*.** **(1.5)**

1. suppl ............... ............... d
2. dec ............... ............... ve
3. bel ............... ............... ve

**B. Add *dis*- or *un*- to the words in the brackets to form their opposites. Then, fill in the blanks.** **(1.5)**

1. The storm caused the Wi-fi to ........................................ (connect) from Ratna's phone.
2. My father bought a ring made of ........................................ (cut) diamonds.
3. On her birthday, Zohra ........................................ (packed) her gifts eagerly.

**C. Look at the picture clues and fill in the blanks.** **(2)**

a. The .....................................  is ..................................... in colour.

b. .....................................  live in ..................................... 

c. Fresh .....................................  and .....................................  keep us healthy.

d. .....................................  and .....................................  keep us fit.

## GRAMMAR ........................................................................................................................ (10)

**A. Underline the verbs in the following sentences.** **(2)**

1. I study well.
2. My dog barked at the stranger.
3. Ravi weighs twenty-eight kilograms.
4. They swam in the swift-flowing river.

**B. Write the past tense for these verbs.** **(2)**

1. worry ..........................................
2. go ..........................................
3. find ..........................................
4. fall ..........................................

**C. Write the simple past tense form of the verbs given in brackets.** **(2)**

1. He .......................................... (hop) on one leg because he was hurt.
2. The clothes .......................................... (dry) quickly because it was a sunny day.
3. The teacher .......................................... (know) who had doodled on the board.
4. The wind .......................................... (blow) so strongly that it turned over the vase.

**D. Fill in the blanks with the present continuous form of the verbs given in brackets.** **(2)**

1. Our family .......................................... (go) on a picnic.
2. My father .......................................... (fry) potatoes to make chips.
3. Andrew .......................................... (write) a story for his little brother.
4. Naina .......................................... (paint) her bedroom wall.

**E. Fill in the blanks with the correct form of the verb given in brackets.** **(2)**

1. Sachin Tendulkar .......................................... (love/hate) cricket.
2. She .......................................... (go/eat) jogging every morning.
3. My cousin Sukhna .......................................... (live/sleep) in Koyamputthoor.
4. The library .......................................... (open/close) at 9 a.m., from Monday to Friday.

# 10 Marco Polo

## READING

**Read the passage and answer the questions.**

Wilbur and Orville Wright were brothers as well as American inventors. They built and flew the first fully functional airplane. In 1878, their father, Milton Wright, bought a small model helicopter for his sons. It was made of cork, bamboo, and paper, and had a rubber band to turn its blades. The Wright brothers got the idea of building an airplane from this toy. They studied birds to understand how they use their wings to balance and control their flight. On 17 December, 1903, they succeeded in flying the first plane.

Many people in America, however, did not believe the brothers had been able to fly a plane. So Wilbur went to Europe hoping that he could convince the people there. He made many public flights there. He also took many important statesmen and journalists on rides. Soon, the Wright brothers became very famous.

*The Wright Brothers' First Flight*

## COMPREHENSION

**A. Mark these sentences as true (T) or false (F).**

1. Wilbur and Orville Wright were American sailors. ☐
2. They got the idea of building an airplane from a toy helicopter. ☐
3. The toy helicopter was made of plastic and wood. ☐
4. The first successful flight took place on 17 December, 1903. ☐
5. The Wright brothers built the first fully functional airplane. ☐

**B. Answer the questions.**

1. What do you know about the model helicopter the Wright brothers got?

   ..........................................................................................

   ..........................................................................................

2. Why did the Wright brothers study birds?

   ..........................................................................................

   ..........................................................................................

3. Why do you think the Wright brothers became famous?

   ..........................................................................................

   ..........................................................................................

4. Write an antonym for each of these words.

   a. important ..............................

   b. success ..............................

## VOCABULARY

**These words have been misspelt. Write their correct spellings in the blanks next to them. Then find the words in the grid.**

1. parashoot ..............................
2. favaer ..............................
3. docter ..............................
4. peiceful ..............................
5. horible ..............................
6. rool ..............................

| | | | | | | | |
|---|---|---|---|---|---|---|---|
| P | E | A | C | E | F | U | L |
| A | G | F | A | V | O | U | R |
| R | F | N | P | I | U | T | U |
| A | B | H | E | W | T | C | L |
| C | O | M | P | U | T | R | E |
| H | O | R | R | I | B | L | E |
| U | W | M | F | S | Q | J | A |
| T | D | O | C | T | O | R | M |
| E | P | I | L | Z | A | M | A |

## Prepositions of place

**Prepositions of place** tell us where someone or something is located. For example:

*Papa is **in** the library.* | *My car is parked **behind** the tree.*

*The dog is hiding **under** the table.* | *I'm waiting **at** the counter.*

Some other common prepositions of place are ***on***, ***opposite***, ***next to***, ***in front of***, ***above***, ***below***, ***between***, ***close to***, ***near***, ***before***, ***outside***, ***inside***, and ***over***.

**A. Look at the picture. Fill in the blanks with the correct prepositions of place.**

1. The mirror is .................................. the washbasin.
2. There is a hairdryer .................................. the shelf.
3. The clothes are .................................. the laundry basket.
4. There are clouds .................................. the window.
5. The curtain hangs .................................. the toilet and the bathtub.
6. There is a mat .................................. the toilet.

## Prepositions of movement

**Prepositions of movement** show the movement of someone or something from one place to another. For example:

*He went **to** the shop.* | *The doctor walked **down** the hall.*

*The children ran **through** the crowd.* | *I strolled **past** the bakery.*

Some other common prepositions of movement are ***off***, ***up***, ***across***, ***along***, ***into***, ***around***, ***under***, ***round***, ***over***, ***from***, ***towards***, and ***back to***.

## B. Fill in the blanks with the correct prepositions from brackets.

1. The old man took a walk .................................. (*in/along/under*) the river.
2. We went .................................. (*over/down/back to*) that temple yesterday.
3. The car stopped .................................. (*around/from/up*) the corner.
4. You may take the book .................................. (*into/from/through*) my table.
5. Will you walk .................................. (*past/above/off*) the market today?
6. You have to go .................................. (*into/in/across*) the bridge.

### Using *Can* and *Can't*

- **Can** is used to show when someone or something is able to do something. It is also used to show the permission to do something.
- **Can't** is the opposite of can. For example:

  *My sister **can** speak French. → My sister **can't** speak French.*

  *You **can** stay up late tonight. → You **can't** stay up late tonight.*

### Using *Must* and *Mustn't*

- **Must** is used when it is necessary for someone to do something. For example:

  *She **must** behave herself.* *You **must** take your medicine.*

- **Mustn't** is used to stop someone from doing something. For example:

  *He **mustn't** run while he's injured.* *You **mustn't** be unkind to animals.*

## C. Fill in the blanks with *can* or *can't*.

1. Peter .................................. play football today. He has fever.
2. My uncle .................................. fly a plane. He is a pilot.
3. Her grandmother .................................. walk. Her knee hurts.
4. I .................................. eat pizza today. It's Sunday!

## D. Fill in the blanks with *must* or *mustn't*.

1. You .................................. brush your teeth every day.
2. You .................................. play with fire.
3. You .................................. fight with your younger brother.
4. You .................................. chew your food properly.

# LISTENING AND SPEAKING

## Listening

**A. Imagine you are travelling in a plane. The air hostess announces some important instructions. Listen to the instructions. Fill in the blanks with the correct words from the box.**

| *upright* | *pleasant* | *switch off* | *welcomed* |
|---|---|---|---|
| *fasten* | *passengers* | *devices* | *New Delhi* |

The air hostess .................................. all the .................................. on the plane. Flight YA 265 is travelling from Hyderabad to ................................... She requested the passengers to keep their seats in an .................................. position for take-off and to .................................. their seat belts. The passengers were instructed to .................................................... their laptops, mobile phones, and other electronic ................................... She wished all the passengers a .................................. journey.

## Speaking

**B. Write down four words that end with *-ance* and four words that end with *-ence*. Now say them out loud. See if you can hear the difference in the way you pronounce them. One has been done for you.**

| *-ance* | *-ence* |
|---|---|
| elegance | evidence |
| .................................. | .................................. |
| .................................. | .................................. |
| .................................. | .................................. |

# WRITING

**Imagine you and your parents are travelling by car to another city. There is loud music playing in the car. There is also a bottle of water and a medicine kit in the car.**
**Suddenly, your mother gets a headache. List down four ways you can help her feel better.**

1. ..............................................................................................................................
2. ..............................................................................................................................
3. ..............................................................................................................................
4. ..............................................................................................................................

# 11 On the Water

## VOCABULARY

**A. Fill in the blanks with the antonyms of the underlined words.**

1. Sheela is tall but Rohan is .......................................
2. The milk is fresh but the bread is .......................................
3. A mouse is tiny but an elephant is .......................................
4. The lane was narrow but the highway was .......................................
5. I lost my pen yesterday, but I ....................................... it today.
6. Grapes are sweet but lemons are .......................................
7. Zeba's desk is neat but Sara's desk is .......................................
8. The manager was very polite but the waiter was .......................................

**B. Fill in the blanks with the help of the picture clues.**

Last year, we went for a cruise on a .......................... . It was a .......................... 

experience. The .......................................  was a jolly man with a thick black ....................... . There was a .................................... 

on the deck. The ship was ..................... 3 storeys high. There were ..............................

 and basketball courts on the ship. It had a ........................  floor too.

## ACTIVITY

**Where did you go on your last vacation? What was the most memorable thing you saw there? Draw it here.**

# 12 The Mouse Maiden

## READING

**Read the passage and answer the questions.**

One day, a very hungry fox set out to look for food in the forest. He came upon a crow sitting on the branch of a tall tree. The crow was holding a big piece of cheese in its beak. 'I don't need to go any further,' thought the sly fox. 'I'll just take the crow's cheese.' The fox called up to the crow. 'Hello! What a beautiful creature you are. You have such shiny feathers, and such pretty wings. I'm sure you have a lovely voice too. Won't you sing a song for me?'

Now, the crow was so pleased by the fox's flattery that it forgot to be careful. So it opened its beak wide to utter its loudest caw, and down fell the cheese straight into fox's open mouth. This was exactly what the fox wanted. 'Thank you,' he said, and ran away. The foolish crow was left with nothing.

## COMPREHENSION

**A. Choose the correct option.**

1. Where did the fox go to look for food?

   a. the swamp

   b. the forest

   c. the lake

2. Which bird did he see in the tree?
   a. a crow
   b. a parrot
   c. a duck
3. What fell into the fox's mouth?
   a. an apple
   b. a fly
   c. cheese
4. What shiny thing did the fox say the crow has?
   a. feathers
   b. beak
   c. eyes

**B. Answer the questions.**

1. Why did the fox decide not to go any further?

   ........................................................................................................

   ........................................................................................................

2. How did the fox flatter the crow?

   ........................................................................................................

   ........................................................................................................

3. Why do you think the crow lost its cheese to the fox? Give a reason for your answer.

   ........................................................................................................

   ........................................................................................................

4. Circle the correct meaning of each of these words/phrases.

   a. deceitful (*dumb* *sly* *honest*)

   b. to give false and untrue praise (*flatter* *applaud* *hail*)

## VOCABULARY

### Sound words

**Sound words** are used to describe the sound a person or thing makes. These words sound the same as they are pronounced. For example:

*The cow **mooed** loudly.* (a *moo* sound)

*He **squished** the sandwiches by sitting on them.* (a *squish* sound)

**Fill in the blanks with the correct sound words in brackets. Do remember to use the correct verb forms.**

1. The .............................. (*tick-tock/lick-lock/tip-top*) of the clock echoed in the silent room.
2. Tom .............................. (*string/swish/slip*) his twig through the air.
3. The race car .............................. (*doom/tune/vroom*) down the track.
4. The soda .............................. (*quiz/fizz/miss*) when he opened the bottle.
5. The snake .............................. (*lisp/toss/hiss*) at the crouching tiger.
6. The pebble fell into the water with a .............................. (*plop/top/stop*).

# GRAMMAR

## Conjunctions

**Conjunctions** are words that are used to join two words or sentences. Words like ***or***, ***because***, ***but***, *and* ***so*** are some common conjunctions. For example:

*Sangita can sing. She can't play the piano. → Sangita can sing* ***but*** *she can't play the piano.*

*I'm happy. I scored good marks. → I'm happy* ***because*** *I scored good marks.*

**A. Fill in the blanks with the correct conjunctions from brackets.**

1. Shimla is cold .............................. (*and/because*) wet in winters.
2. John would like to go .............................. (*but/because*) he can't.
3. Seema was late for work today .............................. (*or/because*) her car broke down.
4. Do you like chocolate .............................. (*or/and*) ice cream better?
5. It was raining .............................. (*but/so*) we decided not to go out.
6. We are not going to the Red Fort .............................. (*or/because*) it is closed today.

## Adverbs of manner

**Adverbs** are words that describe a verb. **Adverbs of manner** tell us *how* (or in what manner) something happens. For example:

*The gymnast* ***jumped lightly*** *over the pole.* (Here, *lightly* tells us how the gymnast jumped.)
*verb adverb*

**B. Fill in the blanks with the correct adverbs of manner from the words in brackets.**

1. She .............................. (*gentle*) closed the door after entering the classroom.
2. Sunil was sitting .............................. (*comfortable*) and didn't want to move.

3. Payal drank the water ........................... (*quick*).
4. The old man spoke ........................... (*kind*) to the frightened child.
5. The little boy kept his books ........................... (*careful*) on the table.
6. He waited ........................... (*patient*) for the bus to arrive.

## LISTENING AND SPEAKING

### Listening

**A. Listen to the passage and fill in the blanks.**

Rohit lives with his parents on a ...................... in ...................... The farm has many ......................, ......................, and cows. Rohit ...................... up early to ...................... all the animals. Every year, Rohit's ...................... cousins visit him in the ...................... They stay for one .................................. Rohit's cousins' names are ...................... and ...................... They come to India from ...................... Rohit likes ...................... a lot because she knows many ...................... and ...................... feed the animals. But ...................... is very proud and ...................... help at all.

### Speaking

#### Homographs

**Homographs** are words that have the same spellings but have different meanings, and are pronounced differently, too. For example:

*The tourists asked the guide to **lead** the way.*

*The **lead** of my pencil is very strong.*

**B. Underline the homographs in these sentences. Then say them out loud to hear the difference in pronunciation.**

1. The nurse wound the bandage around the wound.
2. When I went to live in the jungle, I saw a live elephant.
3. The magician was wearing a bow. He took a bow at the end of his act.
4. The wind blew strongly as she walked down the road that winds through the city.

**C. Sing this poem to your mother or father. Stress on the words with *oo* in them.**

Every time I go to the roof,
I see the owl sitting in the tree.
It's black as soot, soot, soot.

It goes hoot, hoot, hoot.
When I'm in a good mood,
I take my drum to the roof.
And I play a beat that goes boom, boom, boom.
If you want proof,
You have to come and see me soon.

## WRITING

**Imagine you have just met an alien. The alien has special features and a different kind of body. Write a letter to your favourite aunt telling her about the special features of the alien. You may begin like this:**

Dear .................................... (write your aunt's name)

Today I met an alien. It was ..............................................................................................................

..............................................................................................................................................................

..............................................................................................................................................................

..............................................................................................................................................................

..............................................................................................................................................................

..............................................................................................................................................................

..............................................................................................................................................................

..............................................................................................................................................................

..............................................................................................................................................................

..............................................................................................................................................................

..............................................................................................................................................................

..............................................................................................................................................................

..............................................................................................................................................................

..............................................................................................................................................................

With love

.................................... (write your name)

# 13 The Selfish Giant

## READING

**Read the passage and answer the questions.**

Mother Teresa was born in Albania in 1910. Her real name was Agnes. When she was very young, Agnes and her siblings were taught to be charitable by their mother.

When she was 18-years old, Agnes decided she wanted to be a missionary in India. So, she trained to become a nun. She came to India in 1929. Later, she began teaching at a girls' school in Kolkata. She soon learned to speak Bengali and Hindi fluently.

One day, when she was travelling by train, she felt a need to help the poor and sick people living in the slums of Kolkata. Her goal was to help the unwanted, the unloved, and the uncared for. Agnes worked very hard, and eventually opened a school, an orphanage, and a family clinic in the slums. In 1937, she became known as Mother Teresa.

## COMPREHENSION

**A. Choose the correct option.**

1. Where was Agnes born?
   a. India
   b. Albania
   c. Canada
2. What did Agnes decide she wanted to be?
   a. a doctor
   b. a writer
   c. a missionary

3. What did Agnes become known as in 1937?
   a. Mother Teresa
   b. Mother Agnes
   c. Mother Mary
4. How old was Agnes when she decided to become a missionary nun in India?
   a. 21
   b. 17
   c. 18

**B. Answer the questions.**

1. What were Agnes and her siblings taught by their mother?

   ..............................................................................................

   ..............................................................................................

2. What languages did Mother Teresa learn to speak in India?

   ..............................................................................................

   ..............................................................................................

3. What was Mother Teresa's goal?

   ..............................................................................................

   ..............................................................................................

4. Why do you think Mother Teresa opened a school and a clinic in the slums? Give a reason for your answer.

   ..............................................................................................

   ..............................................................................................

5. Write the simple present form of these verbs.

   a. taught ..................................   c. bought ..................................

   b. caught ..................................   d. brought ..................................

## VOCABULARY

### Synonyms

A **synonym** is a word that has the same meaning or nearly the same meaning as another word. For example:

*great – excellent*   *bucket – pail*   *close – near*   *important – vital*   *happy – joyful*

**A. Choose the correct synonyms for these words.**

1. answer
   a. ask — b. reply — c. tell
2. error
   a. harm — b. thin — c. mistake
3. fix
   a. repair — b. stitch — c. hard
4. rush
   a. hurry — b. sell — c. begin
5. help
   a. slim — b. thick — c. aid
6. leave
   a. plan — b. bank — c. depart

## Anagrams

An **anagram** is a type of word play. In this, the order of the letters in a word is changed to make a new word. For example:

The word ***silent*** is changed into the word ***listen*** by rearranging the letters.

Note that the letters in both the words are the same; only their placement is different.

**B. Fill in the blanks to make anagrams for these words. Use the clues provided.**

| | | | |
|---|---|---|---|
| 1. tame | m _ _ t | m _ _ e | t _ _ m |
| 2. limes | m _ _ _ s | s l _ _ e | s _ _ l e |
| 3. items | t _ _ e s | m _ _ e s | e m _ _ s |
| 4. pots | p _ _ t | s _ _ t | t _ _ s |
| 5. live | e _ _ l | v _ _ l | v _ _ e |

# GRAMMAR

## Do/Does/Did

The words ***do***, ***does***, and ***did*** are often used to form simple questions. For example:

*They play Ludo.* (statement) → ***Do** they play Ludo?* (question)

*Sheetal has a book.* (statement) → ***Does** Sheetal have a book?* (question)

*Anuj ate an apple.* (statement) → ***Did** Anuj eat an apple?* (question)

**Rearrange the following words to form questions. Begin each question with *Do/Does/Did*, as required.**

1. go / you / home / tomorrow / want / to

2. the / Sheela / today / market / to / go

3. hotel / the / pets / allow

4. team / your / yesterday / well / play

5. play / children / every day / the / here

6. everyone / chocolate / like / cream / ice

# LISTENING AND SPEAKING

## Listening

**A. Listen to a paragraph and arrange these sentences in the correct order.**

- The National Flag is hoisted. ☐
- This colourful procession ends in the playground. ☐
- Teachers tell students about the importance of the Independence Day. ☐
- We all sing the National Anthem. ☐
- The students and teachers gather for a parade. ☐
- Every year, we celebrate Independence Day in school. ☐
- Everyone takes an oath to respect and serve the country. ☐

## Speaking

**B. Imagine you have to attend a family function in the evening. Request your teacher to allow you to leave early. Role-play the conversation with your friend. Don't forget to use words and phrases such as *may I*, *please*, and *thank you*.**

## WRITING

A. **It's Diwali time! Rani and her mother are at a shop to buy a dress for Rani. They are having a conversation about which dress they should buy. Complete the following dialogue between Rani and her mother by filling in the blanks.**

**Mother**: What kind of a dress ..............................................., Rani?

**Rani**: I ............................................... a nice frock.

**Mother**: What colour ............................................... to buy?

**Rani**: I would like a ...............................................

**Mother**: There is a pink frock! Do ............................................... it?

**Rani**: Yes. It has ............................................... too!

B. **Read the passage given below.**

Sakshi and Sneha are twins. They look alike but their interests and hobbies are very different. The only difference in their appearance is that while Sakshi is tall, Sneha is slightly short. Sakshi likes math and science. She is good at volleyball and tennis. Sneha, on the other hand, is fond of geography and English. Sneha is not very interested in sports. Instead, she is fond of music and painting. Both are good in studies. They both love watching movies and eating Chinese food, too.

**Now, make a list of the similarities and differences in their characters.**

**Similarities:**

| Sakshi | Sneha |
|---|---|
| 1. | 1. |
| 2. | 2. |
| 3. | 3. |

**Differences:**

| Sakshi | Sneha |
|---|---|
| 1. | 1. |
| 2. | 2. |
| 3. | 3. |

# TEST 4

## VOCABULARY ........................................................................................................(5)

**A. Unscramble the word correctly. It will form the synonym of the given word. Write it in the blank.** **(1)**

1. yell houst ........................................
2. end inisfh ........................................

**B. Think of a homograph. It fits in both the blanks.** **(1)**

1. My father gifted me a new ........................................ It writes very well.
2. A pig sty is also called this ........................................

**C. Unscramble the word correctly. It will form the antonym of the given word. Write it in the blank.** **(1)**

1. smooth ourgh ........................................
2. broad rowran ........................................

**D. Underline the words that are spelt incorrectly. Write their correct spellings.** **(1)**

1. Tina is my best freind and she is my nieghbor as well.

   ........................................ ........................................

2. We will vizit the libary together.

   ........................................ ........................................

**E. Read the hints. Then, rearrange the letters to form anagrams.** **(1)**

1. mean ........................................ (a lion has this)
2. last ........................................ (we add it in our food)

## GRAMMAR ........................................................................................................(10)

**A. Read these sentences. Use *do*, *did* and *does* to change them into questions.** **(3)**

1. Ravi likes hip-hop dancing.

   ........................................................................................................

2. John and Naseer play kho kho.

   ........................................................................................................

3. They know the way to the theatre.

   ........................................................................................................

**B. Use the conjunction in brackets to join these sentences.** (2)

1. I want to learn swimming. I want to learn horse riding. (or)

   ..............................................................................................................

2. Jignesh could not go out to play. It was raining. (because)

   ..............................................................................................................

3. Ratul set the alarm at 5 o'clock in the morning. He wanted to wake up early. (as)

   ..............................................................................................................

4. Nilli walked to the baker's store. She bought her favourite cake. (and)

   ..............................................................................................................

**C. Choose the correct preposition and fill in the blank.** (2)

1. They built a bridge .................................... the river.

   a. across

   b. along

   c. down

2. We climbed .................................... the mountain slope.

   a. to

   b. across

   c. down

3. The horse jumped .................................... the fence.

   a. over

   b. in

   c. up

4. Ramabai went .................................... the corner to the stationary.

   a. down

   b. up

   c. round

**D. Form adverbs from the words in the brackets. Then, fill in the blanks.** (3)

1. I walked toward my room .................................... . (lazy)
2. We set off for Ooty .................................... . (cheerful)
3. My father snored .................................... . (loud)
4. The wound began to bleed .................................... . (bad)
5. The nurse rocked the cradle .................................... . (gentle)
6. The weavers weave the clothes .................................... . (nimble)